POLISH COOKBOOK

A Flavorful Journey Through Traditional Polish Cuisine
(2023 Guide for Beginners)

Nina Ferguson

CONTENTS

POLISH COOKBOOK

77 Recipes for Making Traditional Polish Dishes at Home

INTRODUCTION

Food is considered one of the most vital parts of human life worldwide. Many fights and wars have been fought based on food distribution or to rid a country of hunger and poverty. Because food is believed to be very significant for everyone, we must study different cuisines worldwide and how they differ.

Polish cuisine is among the best and healthiest in the world.

This book offers all the information you need about the various components of Polish cuisine. You will learn about the history and origins of Polish cuisine. There are numerous intriguing facts about Polish food that can broaden your understanding of this nutritious and delectable cuisine. According to nutrition and dietetics science, Polish food is considered nutritious and can help the body lose weight. Many more health benefits of Polish food have been covered further in the book.

You may prepare Polish food at home by understanding the ingredients needed to begin cooking. There are numerous health benefits to preparing Polish food at home, and you will learn about all of them when you read this remarkable book. This book offers over 77 distinct breakfast, lunch, supper, dessert, and snack recipes eaten by Poles worldwide. You can immediately begin cooking at home with the precise directions below each dish. So, start reading and cooking right away!

Introduction to Polish Food, Chapter 1

Polish food has emerged as Europe's most essential and healthful cuisine. Polish food has many distinctive flavors, such as mustard plants' bitter taste and fermented baked items' delicious taste. Polish cuisine differs from other European cuisines in that pickles are an essential feature of their meals.

Pierogi, the most famous Polish dish, requires no explanation. Pierogi ruskie, or famous dumplings stuffed with potatoes and cheddar, are the most well-known assortments in Poland and abroad. The most popular meal is pierogi with meat fillings, including pork, ham meat, chicken, and veal, typically topped with bacon. More refined varieties work well with lamb, duck, or goose meat.

1.1 Polish Food History and Origins

Poland is located at the crossroads of European and Asian shipping lines. Dealers from remote terrains used to come to Poland for gold and to trade vibrant flavors and remarkable culinary ideas.

Various influences have resulted in Polish food being incredibly flavorful. It's easy to find indications of Jewish food's exotic, sweet, and spicy flavors. The Lithuanians demonstrated the unique skill of dry-preserving meat to the Poles, offering them dried frankfurters, for example, kindziuk.

Polish people, like Ukrainians, enjoy eating dumplings. French cuisine has influenced Polish delicacies. Poland's cuisine is a savory blend of traditional and modern cultures. Polish people have always had amazing natural things, such as Polish salt, from the renowned mines in Wieliczka and Bochnia near Kraków.

Verifiably, Polish timberlands were abundant in wild animals and nectar-producing honey bees. As a result, Polish food became abundant in honey, and Polish nectar became a sought-after delicacy throughout Europe. Today, honey production is experiencing a rebirth, with multiple great giant beehives producing exceptional nectar in various flavors. It's usually served with curds and cottage cheese.

Much of the wealth of nature may be found in Polish cuisine. Wheat and rye are the most regularly used cereals and have been used for ages to bake magnificent Polish bread. Their cuisines are also well-known for containing fish. The Italian-born Polish Queen Bona Sforza introduced a variety of vegetables to Polish cuisine. They are served raw on a platter of mixed greens or bubbling and topped with margarine-caramelized breadcrumbs. Regardless, our triumph is the large selection of soups, which often includes more than 200 variations. One of the most famous Polish dishes is cucumber pickles. Emerging chefs are fusing traditional and ancient Polish culinary techniques with contemporary culinary patterns, creating unique but classic Polish flavors.

1.2 Interesting Polish Food Facts

Here are some interesting facts regarding Polish cuisine:

Polish cuisine is one of the most exquisite cooking techniques in Europe and the world. Polish cuisine is excellent for those looking for comfort foods. Traditional Polish cuisine is straightforward to prepare and delicious.

Wheat, meat, natural goods, spices, nectar, and tastes were crucial in medieval Polish cuisine. Everything was nearby and outgrew the Polish soil. Polish food was quite spicy and calorific back then.

Meat, fish, and vegetables were salted or dried in the sun. Polish folk frequently used maturation and pickling procedures as well. Many additions from other countries impacted Polish cuisine during the partitions. Finally, Polish cuisine results from the best cooking traditions of adjacent lands.

In Poland, the term "bar" does not have the same connotation as in other nations. Typically, it is a simple milk bar serving traditional Polish fare. As a result, if you ask for the soup of the day in a decent tavern or restaurant, you will almost certainly get one of the numerous Polish soups. If you are looking for silky thin soups, Poland is not the place because almost all traditional soups are pretty thick in texture.

Most Poles are enamored with salted cucumbers and cabbage. When the season for these veggies begins, you may observe people stockpiling them and beginning to complete their pickled technique.

Some meals can be considered the most acclaimed jewels in Poland's gastronomic crown. Typically, the recipes for these foods have been handed down from one generation to the next.

Some recipes come from the imperial courts, where well-known and respected culinary experts idealized them. However, most are recipes consumed by ordinary people and are now associated with Polish folklore.

After learning these fascinating facts, you will undoubtedly want to sample Polish cuisine as soon as possible.

1.3 Polish Foods Based on Nutrition and Dietetics

Agriculture accounts for a sizable portion of the Polish economy. This is an excellent depiction of the Polish diet, with oat grains such as wheat, rye, barley, and buckwheat serving as staples. Similarly, popular foods include potatoes, cucumbers, mushrooms, cabbage, and beetroots. Potatoes are the most common side dish served at a Polish supper.

Quinoa, chia seeds, and goji berries have taken grocery shops worldwide by storm, yet much less appealing food kinds can provide equivalent dietary benefits while also costing less. The following are six superfoods that are incredibly healthy and nutritious and are adored by Polish food lovers:

Chard

Even though beets are more commonly associated with Polish food than their verdant relative, chard has played an essential role in the country's culinary history. Chard is an excellent source of vitamins K, A, E, B2, B6, and C, as well as magnesium, calcium, copper, manganese, potassium, and iron. It is excellent for the glucose guidelines and has moderating properties. After the day, it is wise to include a couple of cups on your dinner plate.

Turnips

If you're looking for a side vegetable to supplement the nutritional value of your meal, go to your local rancher's market. Turnips are high in nutrients such as K, A, C, E, B1, B3, B5, B6, B2, and minerals such as manganese, potassium, magnesium, iron, calcium, and copper and make an excellent snack or cause for a side dish of mixed greens.

Millet

Before potatoes became a side dish on Polish plates, the country's food relied heavily on various groats, including the famously filled millet. Millet has just made a huge comeback. Millet is abundant in B vitamins, calcium, iron, potassium, zinc, and magnesium and is a good source of essential lipids. Its regular usage has been linked to improved heart health, a lower risk of diabetes, and lower cholesterol levels.

Parsley

If you think parsley is just a garnish, you might be surprised to learn that this mild vegetable is packed with cancer-fighting compounds and minerals. There are numerous ways to incorporate parsley into your menu, regardless of whether you prefer the leaves or the root.

Cabbage with salt

Salted cabbage is high in beneficial bacteria that can improve your digestive health. It should be on your grocery list. Polish folks typically eat it with ground carrots and apples to enhance flavor and balance the bitterness of the cabbage.

Berries from Aronia

Everyone has probably realized the health benefits of eating berries by now. However, if blueberries, strawberries, and raspberries have become a kitchen mainstay, it is time to introduce some Aronia berries, also known as chokeberries. Aronia berries enhance blood flow, regulate circulatory strain, and aid in weight loss. They also have anti-inflammatory effects and aid in the health of your urinary system.

All of the ingredients used in Polish cuisine are incredibly healthy, making this meal extremely nutritious.

1.4 Polish Food Preparation at Home

Meal planning and preparation are fantastic skills for your health and fitness toolbox. A well-planned meal plan can help you improve the quality of your diet or achieve a specific health goal while saving you time and money along the way.

Cooking your meals at home will allow you to save time while also improving your health. Many people are so busy with their daily lives that they don't have enough time to cook at home and consume unhealthy foods.

Polish cuisine is straightforward to prepare at home. This cuisine has many recipes, and you will always be energized with it in your entire life. We've simplified cooking at home by including healthy and simple recipes in the chapters below. So, start reading and learning about Polish cuisine today!

The World of Polish Breakfast Recipes, Chapter 2

Polish folks enjoy eating eggs and meat for breakfast. All of the breakfast foods listed below are healthy and traditional in Poland:

Recipe for Polish Scramble with Egg Sausage

Time to Prepare: 30 minutes

Time to cook: 10 minutes

4 servings

Ingredients:

½ cup Polish ground sausage

 salt and pepper

1-ounce butter

1 cup black olives

1 tomato

 6 egg

 1 teaspoon garlic

1 cup red onions

¼ cup chopped cilantro leaves

Instructions:

1. Preheat a frying pan.

2. Melt the butter in the skillet.

3. Stir in the garlic and red onion.

4. Cook the mixture on medium-high heat for several seconds or until it changes color.

5. Stir in the tomatoes and sausage.

6. Cook until they are tender but still a little crunchy.

7. Reduce the heat to low and pour in the beaten eggs, allowing them to set for a few moments.

8. Begin scrambling the egg mixture.

9. Season with salt and pepper.

10. Garnish with cilantro leaves, if desired.

11. Your dish is now ready to serve.

Easter Breakfast in Poland

Time to prepare: 20 minutes

Time to cook: 20 minutes

4 servings

Ingredients:

2 tbsp olive oil

4 eggs

1 cup horseradish root

1 cup Smoked kielbasa

½ cup Fresh kielbasa

1 cup Chopped tomatoes

1 cup Cured chopped ham

1 cup Heavy cream

Salt to taste

Black pepper to taste

Instructions:

1. Begin by preparing a pan.

2. Toss in the diced tomatoes in the pan.

3. Cook until the tomatoes are tender.

4. Stir in the spices.

5. Place all types of meat in the pan.

6. Boil the eggs before peeling them.

7. Finely chop the boiled eggs.

8. Gently fold in the eggs.

9. Cook all of the ingredients thoroughly before adding the cream.

10. Leave the pan covered for 5 minutes.

11. Your dish is now ready to serve.

Recipe for Polish Potato Pancakes

Time to Prepare: 10 minutes

Time to cook: 15 minutes

2 servings

Ingredients:

½ cup Fresh cilantro, half

3 eggs

1 tablespoon baking powder

1 tablespoon cooking oil

½ cup all-purpose flour

½ cup milk

Black pepper to taste

Salt to taste

1 teaspoon vanilla extract

½ cup potatoes

Instructions:

1. Place the eggs in a large mixing dish.

2. Whisk the eggs until they are smooth.

3. Add the remaining ingredients one at a time, being careful not to form any clusters.

4. Finally, add the potatoes, salt, and black pepper.

5. Gently fold in all of the ingredients.

In a pan, heat the cooking oil.

7. Pour some of the pancake mix into the pan and cook it thoroughly.

8. Cook the pancakes till golden brown on both sides.

9. The dish is now ready to serve.

Recipe for Polish Egg and Sausage Stuffed Potatoes

Time to Prepare: 10 minutes

Time to cook: 20 minutes

2 servings

Ingredients:

½ teaspoon Smoked paprika

1 cup Hot sauce

2 cups Ground sausage

2 tablespoons Minced garlic

4 Eggs

1 tablespoon Powdered cumin

Salt to taste

Black pepper to taste

1 cup Red onion

½ cup Cilantro

2 tablespoon Olive oil

4 Small potatoes

1 cup Chopped tomatoes

1 cup Cheese

Instructions:

1. Get a pan.

2. Pour in the oil and onions.

3. Saute the onions until aromatic.

4. Stir in the garlic until it changes color.

5. Stir in the diced tomatoes.

6. Stir in the sausage.

7. Combine the spices, salt, and pepper in a mixing bowl.

8. Allow the mixture to cook for fifteen minutes.

9. Gently fold in the eggs.

10. Bring the mixture to a boil.

11. Scrub the potatoes from the inside out.

12. Combine the cooked mixture with the potatoes.

13. Sprinkle with the shredded cheese.

14 Arrange the potatoes on a baking sheet.

15 Bake the potatoes for 10 minutes at 350°F.

16. Sprinkle with cilantro on top.

17. Your dish is now ready to serve.

Polish Yeast Pancakes Recipe

Time to Prepare: 10 minutes

Time to cook: 15 minutes

2 servings

Ingredients:

3 eggs

1 tablespoon Cooking Oil

½ cup all-purpose flour

½ cup milk

½ cup sugar

½ teaspoon dry yeast

Salt to taste

1 teaspoon Vanilla extract

Instructions:

1. In a large mixing basin, combine the eggs.

2. Whisk the eggs until they are smooth.

3. Add the remaining ingredients one at a time, being careful not to form any clusters.

4. Gently fold in all of the ingredients.

5. Heat the frying oil in a skillet.

6. Pour some of the pancake mix into the pan and cook it thoroughly.

7. Cook the pancakes till golden brown on both sides.

8. The dish is now ready to serve.

Recipe for Zapiekanka (Polish Open Faced Sandwich)

Time to Prepare: 30 minutes

Time to cook: 10 minutes

4 servings

Ingredients:

2 tablespoons mayonnaise

 Salad leaves as needed

½ cup heavy cream

3 tablespoons lemon juice

Asino berries as needed

 Bread slices as needed

1 tablespoon Sugar

Instructions:

1. In a large mixing bowl, combine the mayonnaise, heavy cream, lemon juice, and sugar until well combined.

2. Toast the slices of bread.

3. Arrange the salad leaves on top of the bread slices.

4. Drizzle the mayonnaise, heavy cream, lemon juice, and sugar mixture over the slices.

5. Garnish with asino berries.

6. The dish is now ready to serve.

Recipe for Polish Apple Pancakes

Time to Prepare: 10 minutes

Time to cook: 15 minutes

2 servings

Ingredients:

3 eggs

1 tablespoon Cooking Oil

½ cup all-purpose flour

½ cup milk

½ cup sugar

1/2 teaspoon baking powder

1 cup chopped apple

Salt to taste

1 teaspoon vanilla extract

Instructions:

1. In a large mixing basin, combine the eggs.

2. Whisk the eggs until they are smooth.

3. Add the remaining ingredients one at a time, being careful not to form any clusters.

4. Gently fold in all of the ingredients.

5. Heat the frying oil in a skillet.

6. Pour some of the pancake mix into the pan and cook it thoroughly.

7. Cook the pancakes till golden brown on both sides.

8. The dish is now ready to serve.

Recipe for Polish Breakfast Sandwich

Time to prepare: 30 minutes

Time to cook: 15 minutes

3 servings

Ingredients:

Cheese slices as needed

½ cup Mayonnaise

6 Eggs

4 tablespoons vegetable oil

 1 teaspoon onion

½ teaspoon chopped garlic

2 tablespoons butter

 ½ cup Chopped tomatoes

1 cup kielbasa

Salt to taste

Black pepper to taste

 Bread slices as needed

Instructions:

1. Begin with a big pan.

2. Stir in the onion and butter.

3. Cook the onions until they are tender.

4. Add the minced garlic and chopped tomatoes to the pan.

5. Cook the mixture and then add the kielbasa.

6. Season with salt and pepper on the pan.

7. Cook the mixture thoroughly before serving.

8. Cook the eggs in vegetable oil.

9. Toast the bread pieces and cover each with mayonnaise.

10. Arrange the kielbasa and fried egg on the bread slices.

11. Place another slice of bread on top of the cheese slice.

12. Your dish is now ready to serve.

Recipe for Polish Paczki Donuts

Time to Prepare: 10 minutes

Time to cook: 30 minutes

6 servings

Ingredients:

½ cup butter

8 Eggs

2 cups Sugar

3 cups Flour

1 cup Milk

1 tablespoon baking powder

2 tablespoons Sour cream

1 teaspoon Baking soda

To make the icing:

1 cup mixed berry jam,

1 cup icing sugar

Instructions:

1. In a large mixing basin, thoroughly combine all ingredients.

2. Make a semi-thick dough out of the mixture.

3. Heat the oil in a pan.

4. Using a doughnut cutter, create a spherical doughnut-like structure.

5. Cook the doughnuts in hot oil.

6. Allow the doughnuts to cool.

7. Sprinkle the icing sugar over the doughnuts.

8. Pipe the berry jam between the doughnuts using a pipping bag.

9. Your dish is now ready to serve.

Recipe for Polish Pancakes with Pork and Mushrooms

Time to Prepare: 10 minutes

Time to cook: 15 minutes

2 servings

Ingredients:

½ cup freshly chopped cilantro

3 Eggs

½ cup chopped mushrooms

1 tablespoon baking powder

1 tablespoon cooking oil

½ cup all-purpose flour

½ cup milk

 Black pepper to taste

Salt as needed

½ cup ground pork meat

Instructions:

1. In a large mixing basin, combine the eggs.

2. Whisk the eggs until they are smooth.

3. Add the remaining ingredients one at a time, being careful not to form any clusters.

4. Add the pork meat, mushrooms, salt, and black pepper.

5. Gently fold in all of the ingredients.

In a pan, heat the cooking oil.

7. Pour some of the pancake mix into the pan and cook it thoroughly.

8. Cook the pancakes till golden brown on both sides.

9. The dish is now ready to serve.

Recipe for Polish Sausage Quiche

Time to Prepare: 30 minutes

Time to cook: 10 minutes

4 servings

Ingredients:

2 tbsp. olive oil

 2 Eggs

 ½ cup Milk

Quiche dough as needed

1 cup smoked sausage meat

1 cup chopped tomatoes

Chopped cilantro as needed

1 teaspoon Combine spice powder

1 cup Onion

1 teaspoon Chopped garlic

 ½ teaspoon Smoked paprika

1 cup shredded cheddar cheese

Instructions:

1. Get a pan.

2. Stir in the onion and oil.

3. Cook until the onions are tender and aromatic.

4. Stir in the tomatoes and garlic.

5. Stir in the spices.

6. When the tomatoes are done, mix in the sausage meat.

7. Carefully combine the ingredients and cover the pan.

When the food is entirely cooked, turn off the heat.

9. Stir in the eggs and milk once the mixture has cooled.

10. Place the dough in a baking dish and top with the quiche filling.

11. Sprinkle with the shredded cheddar cheese.

12 Cook the quiche for 20 minutes.

13. Garnish with cilantro.

14. Your dish is now ready to serve.

Recipe for Polish Sausage and Herb Omelet

Time to Prepare: 30 minutes

Time to cook: 10 minutes

4 servings

Ingredients:

¼ cup fresh herbs

2 teaspoons crushed red pepper

½ cup chopped red onions

½ cup Polish sausage slices

season with black pepper to taste

As needed, butter

Season with salt to taste

4 baby plum tomatoes

4 Eggs

½ cup cilantro

Instructions:

1. Take a large mixing dish.

2. Add the eggs, tomatoes, spices, sausage slices, onions, and herbs to the bowl.

3. Melt the butter in a saucepan.

4. Melt the butter in a saucepan.

5. Pour the egg mixture over the pan without mixing.

6. Cook for a few minutes or until the mixture is cooked on the bottom.

7. Turn the omelet over.

8. Serve the omelet with the chopped cilantro on top.

9. The dish is now ready to serve.

Recipe for Polish Potato Oven Omelet

Time to Prepare: 30 minutes

Time to cook: 10 minutes

4 servings

Ingredients:

2 teaspoons crushed red pepper

½ cup chopped red onions

½ cup potato slices

season with black pepper to taste

As needed, butter

Season with salt to taste

4 baby plum tomatoes

4 Eggs

½ cup cilantro

1 cup shredded cheese

Instructions:

1. Take a large mixing dish.

2. Add the eggs, tomatoes, spices, sausage slices, onions, and herbs to the bowl.

3. Melt the butter in a baking dish.

4. Pour the egg mixture into the baking dish and top with the cheese.

5. Bake the omelet for 10 to 15 minutes.

6. Serve the omelet with the chopped cilantro on top.

7. The dish is now ready to serve.

Recipe for Polish Braided Easter Egg Bread

Time to Prepare: 30 minutes

Time to cook: 30 minutes

10 servings

Ingredients:

One-quarter cup of whole milk

1 and ½ cups refined sugar

5-pound bread flour

Season with salt to taste.

1 cup unsalted butter

There are ten eggs.

Water, 2 cups

One egg wash

Two packets of active yeast

Instructions:

1. Combine all of the ingredients in a mixing basin.

2. Combine all of the ingredients in a large mixing bowl.

3. Form the mixture into a dough structure.

4. Form the dough into a log.

5. Cut the log into three strands, each linked at a corner.

6. Braid the dough and set it on a baking sheet that has been buttered.

7. Bake the bread for thirty minutes or until golden brown.

8. Cut the bread into slices.

9. Your dish is now ready to serve.

Recipe for Polish Stuffed Eggs

Time to Prepare: 10 minutes

Time to cook: 20 minutes

2 servings

Ingredients:

smoked paprika, ½ tsp

1 cup hot sauce

2 cups ground sausage

2 tbsp garlic mince

a total of four eggs

1 tablespoon cumin powder

Season with salt to taste.

Black pepper, as desired

1 cup red onion

½ cup cilantro

2 tbsp olive oil

1 cup chopped tomatoes

1 cup shredded cheese

Instructions:

1. Get a pan.

2. Pour in the oil and onions.

3. Saute the onions until aromatic.

4. Stir in the garlic until it changes color.

5. Stir in the diced tomatoes.

6. Stir in the sausage.

7. Combine the spices, salt, and pepper in a mixing bowl.

8. Allow the mixture to cook for fifteen minutes.

9. Boil and peel the eggs.

10. Remove and break the egg yolk.

11. Combine the egg yolk and sausage combination.

12. Combine the two ingredients and fill the boiled eggs with the mixture.

13. Sprinkle with the shredded cheese.

14 Arrange the eggs on a baking sheet.

Bake the eggs for 10 minutes.

16. Sprinkle with cilantro on top.

17. Your dish is now ready to serve.

The World of Polish Lunch Recipes, Chapter 3

Polish recipes frequently include sauerkraut, meats, mushrooms, and cucumbers and are seasoned with various spices and seasonings. Here are some simple recipes that you can make today:

Recipe for Polish Baranina

Time to prepare: 20 minutes
Time to cook: 10 minutes
4 servings

Ingredients:
3 tablespoons fresh chopped cilantro
Season with salt to taste.
Black pepper, as desired
2 teaspoons lemon spice mixture
1 tablespoon capers
One-and-a-half-pound mutton chops
1 teaspoon horseradish
1 cup heavy cream
2 tbsp mayonnaise
1/2 cup dry white wine
1 tablespoon olive oil

Instructions:
1. Combine all of the ingredients in a large mixing dish.
2. Combine everything and make sure the mutton chops are thoroughly coated with the marinade.
3. Preheat the oven to 350°F.
4. Arrange the mutton chops on a baking sheet.
5. Make sure the baking tray is thoroughly oiled.
6. Bake the mutton chops for 10 to 15 minutes.
7. Garnish the chops with fresh cilantro, if desired.
8. The dish is now ready to serve.

Recipe for Polish Potato Soup

Time to Prepare: 30 minutes
Time to cook: 20 minutes
4 servings

Ingredients:
2 tbsp olive oil
four chopped potatoes
1 cup chopped carrots
1/2 cup lime juice
1 cup chopped celery
1 cup chopped tomatoes
1 teaspoon of spice powder
1 cup onion
As needed, chopped fresh parsley
smoked paprika, ½ tsp
1 bay leaf
1 cup chopped bacon
Season with salt to taste.
Black pepper, as desired
2 cups chicken broth

Instructions:
1. Get a pan.
2. Stir in the onion and oil.
3. Cook until the onions are tender and aromatic.
4. Stir in the tomatoes.
5. Stir in the spices.
6. Add the bacon, potatoes, celery, carrots, and stock when the tomatoes have finished cooking.

7. Cook the soup for ten to fifteen minutes on high heat.

8. Sprinkle with parsley on top.

9. Your dish is now ready to serve.

Recipe for Polish Haluski

Time to Prepare: 30 minutes
Time to cook: 15 minutes
4 servings

Ingredients:
1 packet of egg noodles
2 cups sliced green cabbage
1/2 cup chopped parsley
1/2 cup chopped yellow onions
Lemon juice, 2 tbsp
2 tablespoons grated cottage cheese
1 cup bacon slices
As needed, season with salt
two tablespoons butter
as needed, crushed black pepper

Instructions:
1. Begin with a big pan.
2. Stir in the butter and bacon chunks.
3. Fry the bacon slices and then serve.
4. To the pan, add the onions and cabbage.
5. In a separate skillet, bring the noodles to a boil according to package directions.
6. Remove the noodles from the water.
7. Toss the noodles in the pan.

8. Add the remaining ingredients to the pan.
9. Cook for ten to fifteen minutes, depending on the ingredients.
10. Before serving, crumble the cooked bacon slices on top.
11. Your dish is now ready to serve.

Recipe for Polish Pierogi

Time to Prepare: 30 minutes
Time to cook: 30 minutes
4 servings

Ingredients:
Season with salt to taste.
Black pepper, as desired
1 bag of dumpling dough
1 cup sour cream
1 cup chopped chives
1 cup cream cheese
½ cup ricotta cheese
2 tbsp garlic mince
Horseradish, 2 tbsp
½ cup chopped parsley
2 tbsp olive oil

Instructions:
1. Take a large mixing dish.
2. Stir in the sour cream and cream cheese.
3. Whisk together both ingredients until frothy.
4. Stir in the ricotta cheese, minced garlic, and horseradish.

5. Combine all of the ingredients thoroughly.
6. Season with salt and pepper to taste.
7. Make the dumpling dough.
8. Cut circles out of the dough and fill them with the mixture.
9. Roll up the dumplings.
10. Place the dumplings in a big saucepan with boiling water.
11. Cook the pierogi for 5 minutes before draining.
12 Fry the dumplings in olive oil until golden brown on both sides.
13. Plate the pierogi and top with chopped parsley leaves.
14. Your dish is now ready to serve.

Recipe for Polish Sauerkraut and Mushroom Pies

Time to Prepare: 10 minutes
Time to cook: 30 minutes
4 servings

Ingredients:
2 tablespoon sauerkraut, chopped
a ½ cup of butter
Pie dough, as needed
1/2 cup sliced mushrooms
As needed, season with salt
as needed, black pepper
2 teaspoons spice
½ cup parsley
For greasing, use butter.

1 teaspoon minced garlic

Instructions:
1. Melt the butter in a big saucepan.
2. To the pan, add the garlic and seasonings.
3. Add the sauerkraut and cut mushrooms when the garlic turns color.
4. Thoroughly cook the ingredients.
5. Place the pie dough in a pie dish that has been buttered.
6. Top with the sauerkraut and mushroom combination.
7. Bake the dish for ten to fifteen minutes at 350°F.
8. Garnish with parsley, if desired.
9. The dish is now ready to serve.

Recipe for Pulpety (Polish Meatballs)

Time to Prepare: 30 minutes
Time to cook: 20 minutes
4 servings

Ingredients:
2 cups heavy cream
There are two eggs.
Season with salt to taste.
Black pepper, as desired
1 cup of milk
One cup onion
1 cup bread crumbs
2 tablespoons sugar
1 pound minced sausage meat

3 cups of beef stock
1 pound minced beef meat
2 tbsp. minced ginger
a pinch of cayenne pepper
2 tablespoons butter
5 tablespoons all-purpose flour
1 cup chopped dill

Instructions:

1. Take a large mixing dish.
2. To the bowl, add the oil and onions.
3. Place the chopped ginger in the mixing bowl.
4. Place the minced meat and sausage in a mixing dish.
5. Combine the spices, eggs, and bread crumbs in a mixing bowl.
6. Combine all of the ingredients.
7. Make spherical meatballs out of the beef and sausage mixture.
8. Preheat a grill pan.
9. Drizzle with olive oil.
10. Top with the meatballs.
11. Cook the meatballs on each side until golden brown.
12. Fry all of the meatballs and serve them.
13. Combine the remaining ingredients in a big saucepan.
14. Add the potatoes and properly boil them.
15. Combine the meatballs with the mixture.
16. Cook the meatballs until they are dry.
17. The dish is now ready to serve.

Recipe for Mielone (Polish Meat Patties)

Time to Prepare: 25 minutes
Time to cook: 15 minutes
4 servings

Ingredients:

2 teaspoons garlic powder
3 tablespoons chopped red onions
½ cup chopped cilantro
2 cups minced beef meat
2 tablespoons fresh dill, chopped
2 tablespoons vegetable oil
Season with salt to taste
2 cups minced turkey meat
season with black pepper to taste
There are two eggs.
2 tablespoons all-purpose flour
2 teaspoons butter

Instructions:

1. In a large mixing bowl, combine the onions and garlic.
2. Stir in the remaining ingredients.
3. Form the mixture into round patties.
4. Melt the butter and oil in a skillet.
5. Cook the pork patties in hot oil.
6. Remove the patties when they are golden brown on both sides.
7. Garnish with cilantro.

8. You can serve it with whatever sauce you choose.

9. The dish is now ready to serve.

Recipe for Bigos (Polish Hunter's Stew)

Time to Prepare: 10 minutes
Time to cook: 40 minutes
2 servings

Ingredients:

2 cups beef broth
1 teaspoon cumin powder
1 cup onion
½ cup lemon juice
Hunter beef, half a pound
smoked paprika, ½ tsp
2 tbsp garlic mince
½ cup cilantro
2 tbsp olive oil
Water, 2 cups
1 cup heavy cream

Instructions:

1. Get a pan.
2. Stir in the onion and oil.
3. Cook until the onions are tender and aromatic.
4. Stir in the minced garlic and ginger.
5. Cook the mixture and stir in the hunting beef.
6. Pour in the spices and water.
7. Bring the stew to a boil and stir in the cream.

8 Pour in the broth.
9. Carefully combine the ingredients and cover the pan.
10. Garnish with cilantro.
11. Your dish is now ready to serve.

Recipe for Salatka Jarzynows (Polish Veggie Salad)

Time to Prepare: 30 minutes
Time to Cook: 15 minutes
4 servings

Ingredients:
2 cups cooked peas
1/2 cup cilantro
1 cup cooked chopped carrots
1/2 cup cubed pickles
1 cup chopped hard-cooked eggs
2 cup mayonnaise
1/2 cup chopped parsley
Season with salt to taste.
1 cup chopped onion
to taste, crushed black pepper
1 cup chopped apples
1 cup chopped cooked potatoes
1/2 cup chopped chives

Instructions:
1. Take a large mixing dish.
2. To the bowl, add the salt, black pepper, and mayonnaise.

3. Whisk the mayonnaise until it becomes frothy.
4. In a separate bowl, combine the remaining ingredients.
5. Combine the ingredients thoroughly.
6. Pour the mayonnaise mixture over the remaining ingredients.
7. Stir until the mayonnaise mixture is evenly coated on the fruits and veggies.
8. Your dish is now ready to serve.

Recipe for Polish Chickpeas

Time to Prepare: 10 minutes
Time to cook: 20 minutes
4 servings

Ingredients:
1 tablespoon garlic
1 bunch of bay leaves
2 teaspoons all spice powder
1 tablespoon black pepper
1 cup smoked bacon
1 teaspoon dried marjoram
Eight dried chilies
½ cup smoked sausage
½ cup chopped red onion
1 pound canned chickpeas
1 cup passata paste
2 tablespoons vegetable oil
garnished with chopped cilantro leaves
Season with salt to taste.

Instructions:

1. Begin with a big pan.
2. Heat the oil and onions in a pan.
3. Cook until the onions are tender and transparent.
4. Place the garlic cloves in the pan.
5. Thoroughly cook the mixture.
6. Combine the passata paste and spices in a mixing bowl.
7. Cook for 5 minutes with the mixture.
8. Toss in the smoked bacon and sausage.
9. Cook the ingredients thoroughly.
10. Stir in the remaining ingredients.
11 Cook for 10 minutes with the pan covered.
12. Garnish with cilantro leaves, if desired.
13. Your meal is now ready to serve.

Recipe for Polish Golonka

Time to Prepare: 10 minutes
Time to cook: 20 minutes
4 servings

Ingredients:

1 tablespoon garlic
1 bunch of bay leaves
2 teaspoons all spice powder
1 tablespoon black pepper
1 cup raw honey
1 teaspoon dried marjoram
8 dried chilies
½ cup cooking beer
½ cup chopped red onion

1 pound ham hock
1 cup beef stock
2 tablespoons vegetable oil
garnished with chopped cilantro leaves
Season with salt to taste.

Instructions:
1. Begin with a big pan.
2. Heat the oil and onions in a pan.
3. Cook until the onions are tender and transparent.
4. Place the garlic cloves in the pan.
5. Thoroughly cook the mixture.
6. Add the seasonings and beef stock.
7. Cook for 5 minutes with the mixture.
8. Pour in the cooking beer and honey.
9. Cook the ingredients thoroughly.
10. Stir in the remaining ingredients.
11 Cook for 10 minutes with the pan covered.
12. Garnish with cilantro leaves, if desired.
13. Your meal is now ready to serve.

Recipe for Polish Gulasz

Time to Prepare: 10 minutes
Time to cook: 20 minutes
4 servings

Ingredients:
1 tablespoon garlic
1 bunch of bay leaves
2 teaspoons all-spice powder

1 tablespoon black pepper
1 cup bell pepper
3 tablespoons all-purpose flour
½ cup tomato paste
½ cup dry red wine
½ cup chopped red onion
1 pound ground pork
1 cup cold water
½ cup beef broth
2 tablespoons vegetable oil
garnished with chopped cilantro leaves
Season with salt to taste.

Instructions:

1. Begin with a big pan.
2. Heat the oil and onions in a pan.
3. Cook until the onions are tender and transparent.
4. Place the garlic cloves in the pan.
5. Thoroughly cook the mixture.
6. Stir in the tomato paste and seasonings.
7. Cook for 5 minutes with the mixture.
8. Pour in the heated red wine and beef broth.
9. Cook the ingredients thoroughly.
10. Combine the flour, bell peppers, ground pork, and cold water in a mixing bowl.
11 Cook for 10 minutes with the pan covered.
12. Garnish with cilantro leaves, if desired.
13. Your meal is now ready to serve.

Recipe for Polish Roasted Duck with Apples

Time to prepare: 20 minutes

Time to cook: 10 minutes
4 servings

Ingredients:
3 tablespoons fresh chopped cilantro
Season with salt to taste.
Black pepper, as desired
2 teaspoons lemon spice mixture
1 tablespoon capers
1 ½ pounds of duck flesh
1 teaspoon horseradish
1 cup dried marjoram
2 tbsp caraway seeds
½ pound little potatoes
1 tablespoon olive oil
1 pound apple cubes

Instructions:
1. Combine all of the ingredients in a large mixing dish.
2. Combine everything and make sure the duck flesh is thoroughly coated with the marinade.
3. Preheat the oven to 350°F.
4. Arrange the duck flesh on a baking sheet.
5. Make sure the baking tray is thoroughly oiled.
6. Bake the duck flesh for 10 to 15 minutes.
7. Garnish with fresh cilantro, if desired.
8. The dish is now ready to serve.

Recipe for Polish Vegan Pierogi with Mushroom Filling

Time to Prepare: 30 minutes
Time to cook: 30 minutes
4 servings

Ingredients:

Season with salt to taste.
Black pepper, as desired
1 bag of dumpling dough
1 cup sour cream
1 cup chopped chives
1 cup sliced mushrooms
2 tbsp garlic mince
Horseradish, 2 tbsp
1/2 cup chopped parsley
2 tbsp olive oil

Instructions:

1. Take a large mixing dish.
2. Stir in the sour cream.
3. Whip the cream until it is frothy.
4. Stir in the cut mushrooms, minced garlic, and horseradish.
5. Combine all of the ingredients thoroughly.
6. Season with salt and pepper to taste.
7. Make the dumpling dough.
8. Cut circles out of the dough and fill them with the mixture.
9. Roll up the dumplings.
10. Place the dumplings in a big saucepan with boiling water.
11. Cook the pierogi for 5 minutes before draining.

12 Fry the dumplings in olive oil until golden brown on both sides.

13. Plate the pierogi and top with chopped parsley leaves.

14. Your dish is now ready to serve.

Recipe for Polish Casserole

Time to prepare: 20 minutes
Time to cook: 20 minutes
4 servings

Ingredients:
2 tbsp olive oil
1 cup Swiss cheese
½ cup of milk
1 cup uncooked penne pasta
1 cup condensed cream
1 teaspoon spice powder
1 cup onion
1 cup sauerkraut
1 teaspoon Dijon mustard
As needed, fresh cilantro, chopped
smoked paprika, ½ tsp
1 cup of kielbasa
1 cup Polish sausage

Instructions:
1. Get a pan.
2. Stir in the onion and oil.
3. Cook until the onions are tender and aromatic.
4. Add the tomatoes to the skillet.

5. Stir in the spices.
6. Carefully combine the ingredients and cover the pan.
7. Combine the Polish sausage and kielbasa in a mixing bowl.
Cook the sausage and kielbasa until done.
9. Turn off the stove.
When the mixture has cooled, add the other ingredients.
11. Transfer the casserole ingredients to a baking dish.
12. Top with the shredded Swiss cheese.
13 Cook the casserole for 20 minutes.
14. When the dish is finished, remove it from the oven.
15. Garnish with cilantro.
Your dish is now ready to serve.

The World of Polish Dinner Recipes, Chapter 4

Polish dinner recipes are well-known worldwide for their enthralling tastes and nutritional content. The following are some delicious and healthy Polish dinner recipes that you should try at home:

Recipe for Polish Stuffed Cabbage

Time to Prepare: 10 minutes

Time to cook: 30 minutes

4 servings

Ingredients:

2 tablespoons red chili pepper

a 1⁄2 cup of butter

As needed, cabbage sheets

1 cup ground beef

1 cup ground pork

1⁄2 cup chopped red onions

1⁄2 cup of milk

1 cup cooked rice

1 teaspoon garlic mince

Tomatoes, 1 cup

1 tablespoon all-spice mix

1 cup mixed cheese

1 cup sour cream

As needed, chopped fresh parsley

1 cup beef stock

Instructions:

1. Begin with a big pan.

2. Melt the butter and add the onions to the pan.

3. To the pan, add the spices and tomatoes.

4. Thoroughly cook the mixture.

5. Stir in the beef mince and pork mince.

6. Add the beef stock and cover the pan to allow the meat to simmer completely.

7. Add the cooked rice and sour cream when the meat mixture has dried out.

8. Spread the prepared mixture over the cabbage sheets and roll them up.

9. Arrange the rolls in a baking pan.

10. Pour the milk over the buns.

11. Sprinkle with the cheese mixture.

12 Bake the mixture for 15 minutes or until the cheese is golden brown.

13. Sprinkle with fresh parsley, if using.

14 The food is now ready to serve.

Recipe for Polish Zurek Soup

Time to Prepare: 30 minutes

Time to cook: 20 minutes

4 servings

Ingredients:

2 tbsp olive oil

2 cups chopped sausage

1 cup chopped carrots

½ cup lime juice

There are 2 eggs.

1 teaspoon dried marjoram

1 cup chopped celery

1 cup chopped parsnip

1 cup chopped tomatoes

½ cup dried berries

5 tablespoons rye flour

One teaspoon of spice powder

1 cup onion

As needed, chopped fresh parsley

smoked paprika, ½ tsp

1 bay leaf

1 cup chopped bacon

Season with salt to taste.

Black pepper, as desired

As needed, Polish bread

2 cups beef broth

Instructions:

1. Get a pan.

2. Stir in the onion and oil.

3. Cook until the onions are tender and aromatic.

4. Stir in the tomatoes.

5. Stir in the spices.

6. Once the tomatoes are done, add the bacon, parsnips, sausages, celery, carrots, and stock.

7. Cook the soup for ten to fifteen minutes on high heat.

8. Stir in the rye flour and the remaining ingredients.

9. Separately boil and peel the eggs in a saucepan.

10. Ensure that the eggs are hard-boiled.

11 Slice them and serve with the soup.

12. Sprinkle with parsley on top.

13 Serve the soup with crusty bread.

14. Your dish is now ready to serve.

Recipe for Polish Potato Dumplings

Time to Prepare: 30 minutes

Time to Cook: 30 minutes

4 servings

Ingredients:

Season with salt to taste.

Black pepper, as desired

1 bag of dumpling dough

1 cup sour cream

1 cup chopped chives

1 cup chopped potatoes

1/2 cup Swiss cheese

2 tbsp garlic mince

Horseradish, 2 tbsp

1/2 cup chopped parsley

2 tbsp olive oil

Instructions:

1. Take a large mixing dish.

2. Stir in the sour cream.

3. Beat the ingredients together until frothy.

4. Stir in the potatoes, Swiss cheese, minced garlic, and horseradish.

5. Combine all of the ingredients thoroughly.

6. Season with salt and pepper to taste.

7. Make the dumpling dough.

8. Cut circles out of the dough and fill them with the mixture.

9. Roll up the dumplings.

10. Place the dumplings in a big saucepan with boiling water.

11. Cook the pierogi for 5 minutes before draining.

12 Fry the dumplings in olive oil until golden brown on both sides.

13. Plate the pierogi and top with chopped parsley leaves.

14. Your dish is now ready to serve.

Recipe for Ryba Smazona (Polish Fried Fish)

Time to Prepare: 10 minutes

Time to cook: 30 minutes

2 servings

Ingredients:

1 pound filets of cod

One tablespoon orange juice

1 tsp garlic powder

12 cup lemon juice

1 cup bread crumbs

a single egg

1 tablespoon chili powder

1 cup olive oil

1 tablespoon cilantro

Parsley, chopped as needed

Season with salt to taste

season with pepper to taste

Cooking oil, as needed

Instructions:

1. Wash and dry the cod filets.

2. Collect a small bowl.

3. Pour in the orange, garlic powder, and lemon juice.

4. Season with chili powder and pepper.

5. Stir in the cilantro until fully combined.

6. Combine all of the ingredients to make a homogeneous paste.

7. Separate the eggs and place them in a separate bowl.

8. Stir in the cod filets and coat thoroughly.

9. Dip the filets of cod into the egg mixture.

10. Roll the filets in the bread crumbs to coat.

11. Fry the cod filets in hot oil.

12. Serve your fish after it has turned golden brown.

13. Garnish with fresh chopped parsley.

14. Your dish is now ready to serve.

Recipe for Polish Broccoli Kopytka

Time to Prepare: 10 minutes

Time to cook: 20 minutes

4 servings

Ingredients:

1 tablespoon garlic

One bunch of bay leaves

2 teaspoons all spice powder

1 tablespoon black pepper

1 cup smoked bacon

1 cup Terderstem

1 teaspoon dried marjoram

Eight dried chilies

1/2 cup smoked sausage

1/2 cup chopped red onion

1 pound broccoli florets

1 cup passata paste

2 tablespoons vegetable oil

garnished with chopped cilantro leaves

Season with salt to taste.

1 cup mashed potatoes (for serving)

Instructions:

1. Begin with a big pan.

2. Heat the oil and onions in a pan.

3. Cook until the onions are tender and transparent.

4. Place the garlic cloves in the pan.

5. Thoroughly cook the mixture.

6. Combine the passata paste and spices in a mixing bowl.

7. Cook for 5 minutes with the mixture.

8. Toss in the smoked bacon and sausage.

9. Cook the ingredients thoroughly.

10. Stir in the remaining ingredients.

11 Cook for 10 minutes with the pan covered.

12. Serve with mashed potatoes on the side and garnish with chopped cilantro leaves.

13. Your meal is now ready to serve.

Recipe for Polish Smothered Chicken

Time to Prepare: 30 minutes

Time to cook: 15 minutes

4 servings

Ingredients:

1 cup portobello mushrooms

1 cup sliced mozzarella cheese

1/2 cup Cajun seasoning

1/2 cup vegetable cream cheese

Lemon juice, 2 tbsp

1 cup bacon strips

1 pound skinless chicken breast

As needed, season with salt

two tablespoons butter

as needed, crushed black pepper

1 teaspoon oregano

1 tsp garlic powder

Instructions:

1. Begin with a big pan.

2. Stir in the butter and bacon chunks.

3. Fry the bacon slices and then serve.

4. Stir in the chicken and garlic powder.

5. Pour in the Cajun seasoning and mix well.

6. Add the remaining ingredients to the pan.

7. Cook for ten to fifteen minutes, depending on the ingredients.

8. Before serving, crumble the cooked bacon slices over the top.

9. Your dish is now ready to serve.

Recipe for Polish Sausage Pierogi

Time to Prepare: 30 minutes

Time to cook: 30 minutes

4 servings

Ingredients:

Season with salt to taste.

Black pepper, as desired

1 bag of dumpling dough

1 cup sour cream

1 cup chopped chives

1 cup chopped Polish sausages

1/2 cup Swiss cheese

2 tbsp garlic mince

Horseradish, 2 tbsp

1/2 cup chopped parsley

2 tbsp olive oil

Instructions:

1. Take a large mixing dish.

2. Stir in the sour cream.

3. Beat the ingredients together until frothy.

4. Combine the chopped Polish sausages, Swiss cheese, minced garlic, and grated horseradish in a mixing bowl.

5. Combine all of the ingredients thoroughly.

6. Season with salt and pepper to taste.

7. Make the dumpling dough.

8. Cut circles out of the dough and fill them with the mixture.

9. Roll up the dumplings.

10. Place the dumplings in a big saucepan with boiling water.

11. Cook the pierogi for 5 minutes before draining.

12 Fry the dumplings in olive oil until golden brown on both sides.

13. Plate the pierogi and top with chopped parsley leaves.

14. Your dish is now ready to serve.

Recipe for Polish Sausage Pierogi

Time to Prepare: 30 minutes

Time to cook: 30 minutes

4 servings

Ingredients:

Season with salt to taste.

Black pepper, as desired

1 bag of dumpling dough

1 cup sour cream

1 cup chopped chives

1 cup chopped Polish sausages

1/2 cup Swiss cheese

2 tbsp garlic mince

Horseradish, 2 tbsp

1/2 cup chopped parsley

2 tbsp olive oil

Instructions:

1. Take a large mixing dish.

2. Stir in the sour cream.

3. Beat the ingredients together until frothy.

4. Combine the chopped Polish sausages, Swiss cheese, minced garlic, and grated horseradish in a mixing bowl.

5. Combine all of the ingredients thoroughly.

6. Season with salt and pepper to taste.

7. Make the dumpling dough.

8. Cut circles out of the dough and fill them with the mixture.

9. Roll up the dumplings.

10. Place the dumplings in a big saucepan with boiling water.

11. Cook the pierogi for 5 minutes before draining.

12. Cook the dumplings in olive oil until golden brown on both sides.

13. Plate the pierogi and top with chopped parsley leaves.

14. Your dish is now ready to serve.

Recipe for Wolowina Pieczona (Polish Roasted Beef)

Time to prepare: 20 minutes

Time to cook: 10 minutes

4 servings

Ingredients:

3 tablespoons fresh chopped cilantro

Season with salt to taste.

Black pepper, as desired

2 teaspoons lemon spice mixture

one-half cup red wine

One and a half pounds of beef meat

1 teaspoon horseradish

1 cup dried marjoram

2 tbsp caraway seeds

Half pound little potatoes

1 tablespoon olive oil

Instructions:

1. Combine all of the ingredients in a large mixing dish.

2. Combine everything and make sure the beef flesh is thoroughly coated with the marinade.

3. Preheat the oven to 350°F.

4. Arrange the beef meat on a baking sheet.

5. Make sure the baking tray is thoroughly oiled.

6. Bake the beef steak for 10 to 15 minutes.

7. Garnish with fresh cilantro, if desired.

8. The dish is now ready to serve.

Recipe for Schab Faszerowany (Polish Stuffed Loin)

Time to Prepare: 30 minutes

Time to cook: 20 minutes

4 servings

Ingredients:

One can find golden fruits.

2 cups bread crumbs

1 teaspoon garlic mince

1 teaspoon orange zest

1/2 cup dried cranberries

1 cup sour cream

2-pound pork loins

1 cup dry white wine

one tablespoon dried thyme

1 tablespoon salted butter

a quarter cup cilantro

1 teaspoon clove powder

to taste, crushed black pepper

Season with salt to taste.

Instructions:

1. Begin with a small pan.

2. Pour in the butter.

3. Place the garlic cloves in the pan.

4. Stir in the cut apples and sour cream.

5. Stir in the dried cranberries and orange zest.

6. Add the bread crumbs and thoroughly combine the ingredients.

7. Stuff the pork loins with the filling and sprinkle the spices.

8. Roast the loins for 15 to 20 minutes.

9. Before serving, sprinkle with cilantro.

10. Your dish is now ready to serve.

Polish Sirloin Beef Recipe

Time to Prepare: 10 minutes

Time to cook: 20 minutes

4 servings

Ingredients:

1 tablespoon garlic

One bunch of bay leaves

2 teaspoons all spice powder

1 tablespoon black pepper

1 teaspoon dried marjoram

Eight dried chilies

1 pound beef sirloin

1/2 cup chopped red onion

1 cup passata paste

2 tablespoons vegetable oil

garnished with chopped cilantro leaves

Season with salt to taste.

Instructions:

1. Begin with a big pan.

2. Heat the oil and onions in a pan.

3. Cook until the onions are tender and transparent.

4. Place the garlic cloves in the pan.

5. Thoroughly cook the mixture.

6. Combine the passata paste and spices in a mixing bowl.

7. Cook for 5 minutes with the mixture.

8. Transfer the beef sirloin to the pan.

9. Cook the ingredients thoroughly.

10. Stir in the remaining ingredients.

11 Cook for 10 minutes with the pan covered.

12. Garnish with cilantro leaves, if desired.

13. Your meal is now ready to serve.

Recipe for Polish Ground Meat Roast

Time to prepare: 20 minutes

Time to cook: 10 minutes

4 servings

Ingredients:

3 tablespoons fresh chopped cilantro

Season with salt to taste.

Black pepper, as desired

2 teaspoons lemon spice mixture

one-half cup red wine

one and a half pounds ground pork meat

1 teaspoon horseradish

1 cup dried marjoram

2 tbsp caraway seeds

one and a half pounds ground beef meat

1 pound ground veal flesh

1 tablespoon olive oil

2 cups mixed cheese

Instructions:

1. Combine all of the ingredients in a large mixing dish.

2. Combine everything and make sure the meat is thoroughly coated with the marinade.

3. Preheat the oven to 350°F.

4. Place the meat on a baking sheet.

5. Make sure the baking tray is thoroughly oiled.

6. Sprinkle with the cheese.

7. Roast the meat for 10 to 15 minutes.

8. Garnish with fresh cilantro, if desired.

9. The dish is now ready to serve.

Recipe for Polish Pork Roast with Wine

Time to prepare: 20 minutes
Time to cook: 10 minutes

4 servings

Ingredients:

3 tablespoons fresh chopped cilantro

Season with salt to taste.

Black pepper, as desired

2 teaspoons lemon spice mixture

one-half cup red wine

1 1/2 pounds of pork meat

1 teaspoon horseradish

1 cup dried marjoram

2 tbsp caraway seeds

1 tablespoon olive oil

Instructions:

1. Combine all of the ingredients in a large mixing dish.

2. Combine everything and make sure the pig meat is thoroughly coated with the marinade.

3. Preheat the oven to 350°F.

4. Arrange the pork meat on a baking sheet.

5. Make sure the baking tray is thoroughly oiled.

6. Roast the pork loin for 10 to 15 minutes.

7. Garnish with fresh cilantro, if desired.

8. The dish is now ready to serve.

Recipe for Losos (Polish Baked Salmon)

Time to Prepare: 10 minutes

Time to cook: 25 minutes

2 servings

Ingredients:

1 tablespoon cumin powder

Season with salt to taste.

Black pepper, as desired

1 tsp turmeric powder

One cup onion

smoked paprika, 1/2 tsp

1/2 cup Dijon mustard

1 pound salmon chunks

2 tbsp garlic mince

2 tbsp. minced ginger

½ cup cilantro

2 tbsp olive oil

3 tablespoons all-purpose flour

Instructions:

1. Take a large mixing dish.

2. To the bowl, add the oil and onions.

3. Stir in the chopped garlic and ginger.

4. Place the tomatoes in the mixing bowl.

5. Stir in the spices.

6. Stir in the cilantro.

7. Combine all of the ingredients.

8. Combine the ingredients, beginning with the all-purpose flour.

9. Spread the mixture over the fish pieces.

Bake the salmon chunks for 10 minutes.

11. Serve them after they are fully cooked.

12. Garnish with cilantro and sliced almonds.

13. You can serve it with any sauce you choose.

14. Your dish is now ready to serve.

Recipe for Polish Meat Cutlets

Time to Prepare: 25 minutes

Time to cook: 15 minutes

4 servings

Ingredients:

2 teaspoons garlic powder

3 tablespoons chopped red onions

1/2 cup chopped cilantro

2 cups minced veal meat

2 tablespoons fresh dill, chopped

2 tablespoons vegetable oil

Season with salt to taste

2 cups minced turkey meat

season with black pepper to taste

There are two eggs.

2 teaspoons butter

Instructions:

1. In a large mixing bowl, combine the onions and garlic.

2. Stir in the remaining ingredients, excluding the eggs.

3. Form the mixture into round cutlets.

4. Melt the butter and oil in a skillet.

5. In a mixing dish, whisk together the eggs.

6. Coat the cutlets with the egg mixture.

7. Fry the pork cutlets in hot oil.

8. Remove the cutlets from the pan when the patties are golden brown on all sides.

9. Garnish with cilantro.

10. The dish is now ready to serve.

Recipe for Polish Roasted Grilled Ribs

Time to prepare: 20 minutes

Time to cook: 10 minutes

4 servings

Ingredients:

3 tablespoons fresh chopped cilantro

Season with salt to taste.

Black pepper, as desired

2 teaspoons lemon spice mixture

one-half cup red wine

One and a half pounds of beef meat

1 teaspoon horseradish

1 cup dried marjoram

2 tbsp caraway seeds

½ lb little potatoes

1 tablespoon olive oil

Instructions:

1. Combine all of the ingredients in a large mixing dish.

2. Combine everything thoroughly and coat the ribs thoroughly with the marinade.

3. Preheat the grill pan.

4. Arrange the ribs on a grill pan.

5. Make sure to oil the pan with butter properly.

6. Grill the ribs for 10 to 15 minutes on each side.

7. Garnish with fresh cilantro, if desired.

8. The dish is now ready to serve.

Recipe for Polish Fish with Root Vegetable

Time to Prepare: 10 minutes

Time to cook: 25 minutes

2 servings

Ingredients:

1 tablespoon cumin powder

Season with salt to taste.

Black pepper, as desired

1 tsp turmeric powder

One cup onion

smoked paprika, 1/2 tsp

1 pound of filet mignon

2 tbsp garlic mince

2 cups root veggies

2 tbsp. minced ginger

½ cup cilantro

2 tbsp olive oil

Instructions:

1. Take a large mixing dish.

2. To the bowl, add the oil and onions.

3. Stir in the chopped garlic and ginger.

4. Stir in the spices.

5. Stir in the cilantro.

6. Combine all of the ingredients.

7. Place the fish pieces in a pan with the mixture.

8. Prepare the fish pieces.

9. Toss in the root veggies in the pan.

10. When thoroughly cooked, serve them.

11 Garnish with cilantro if desired.

12. Your dish is now ready to serve.

Recipe for Polish Beet Soup

Time to Prepare: 30 minutes

Time to cook: 20 minutes

4 servings

Ingredients:

2 tbsp olive oil

1 cup chopped carrots

1/2 cup lime juice

1 cup chopped celery

1 cup chopped tomatoes

One teaspoon spice powder

One cup onion

As needed, chopped fresh parsley

smoked paprika, 1/2 tsp

One bay leaf

1 cup sliced beetroot

Season with salt to taste.

Black pepper, as desired

2 cups vegetable broth

Instructions:

1. Get a pan.

2. Stir in the onion and oil.

3. Cook until the onions are tender and aromatic.

4. Stir in the tomatoes.

5. Stir in the spices.

When the tomatoes are done, add the beets, celery, carrots, and stock.

7. Cook the soup for ten to fifteen minutes on high heat.

8. Sprinkle with parsley on top.

9. Your dish is now ready to serve.

Recipe for Polish Kielbasa Sausage

Time to Prepare: 10 minutes

Time to cook: 20 minutes

4 servings

Ingredients:

1 tablespoon garlic

One bunch of bay leaves

2 teaspoons all spice powder

1 tablespoon black pepper

One cup of kielbasa

1 teaspoon dried marjoram

1/2 cup cooking beer

1/2 cup chopped red onion

1 pound Polish sausage

2 tablespoons vegetable oil

garnished with chopped cilantro leaves

Season with salt to taste.

Instructions:

1. Begin with a big pan.

2. Heat the oil and onions in a pan.

3. Cook until the onions are tender and transparent.

4. Place the garlic cloves in the pan.

5. Thoroughly cook the mixture.

6. Stir in the spices.

7. Cook for 5 minutes with the mixture.

8. Pour in the cooking beer, sausage, and kielbasa.

9. Cook the ingredients thoroughly.

10. Add the remaining ingredients to the pan.

11 Cook for 10 minutes with the pan covered.

12. Garnish with cilantro leaves, if desired.

13. Your meal is now ready to serve.

Recipe for Polish Cheese and Bacon Pierogi

Time to Prepare: 30 minutes

Time to cook: 30 minutes

4 servings

Ingredients:

Season with salt to taste.

Black pepper, as desired

1 bag of dumpling dough

1 cup sour cream

1 cup chopped chives

1 cup chopped bacon

1/2 cup mozzarella cheese

2 tbsp garlic mince

Horseradish, 2 tbsp

1/2 cup chopped parsley

2 tbsp olive oil

Instructions:

1. Take a large mixing dish.

2. Stir in the sour cream.

3. Beat the ingredients together until frothy.

4. Combine the diced bacon, mozzarella cheese, minced garlic, and grated horseradish in a mixing bowl.

5. Combine all of the ingredients thoroughly.

6. Season with salt and pepper to taste.

7. Make the dumpling dough.

8. Cut circles out of the dough and fill them with the mixture.

9. Roll up the dumplings.

10. Place the dumplings in a big saucepan with boiling water.

11. Cook the pierogi for 5 minutes before draining.

12 Fry the dumplings in olive oil until golden brown on both sides.

13. Plate the pierogi and top with chopped parsley leaves.

14. Your dish is now ready to serve.

Recipe for Polish Beef Goulash

Time to Prepare: 10 minutes

Time to cook: 20 minutes

4 servings

Ingredients:

1 tablespoon garlic

One bunch of bay leaves

2 teaspoon all spice powder

1 tablespoon black pepper

1 cup bell pepper

3 tablespoons all-purpose flour

1/2 cup tomato paste

1/2 cup dry red wine

1/2 cup chopped red onion

1 pound ground beef

1 cup cold water

Half cup beef broth

2 tablespoons vegetable oil

garnished with chopped cilantro leaves

Season with salt to taste.

Instructions:

1. Begin with a big pan.

2. Heat the oil and onions in a pan.

3. Cook until the onions are tender and transparent.

4. Place the garlic cloves in the pan.

5. Thoroughly cook the mixture.

6. Stir in the tomato paste and seasonings.

7. Cook for 5 minutes with the mixture.

8. Pour in the heated red wine and beef broth.

9. Cook the ingredients thoroughly.

10. Combine the flour, bell peppers, ground beef, and cold water in a mixing bowl.

11 Cook for 10 minutes with the pan covered.

12. Garnish with cilantro leaves, if desired.

13. Your meal is now ready to serve.

The World of Polish Dessert Recipes, Chapter 5

Polish sweets are exceptionally delicious and healthful, and you should try all sixteen of these delectable recipes at home because they are simple to prepare and will undoubtedly brighten your day:

Recipe for Polish Coffee Cake

Time to Prepare: 10 minutes

Time to cook: 30 minutes

2 servings

Ingredients:

1/2 teaspoon cinnamon powder

a half cup of coffee

1 teaspoon yeast

1 cup self-rising flour

1 teaspoon mixed spice

1 tablespoon milk

a teaspoon baking powder

There are two eggs.

a ½ cup of butter

1 cup brown sugar

1/2 cup orange zest

Instructions:

1. Get a pan.

2. Pour in the water.

3. Stir in the yeast and cook it.

4. Turn off the stove.

5. Pour the milk into a separate basin.

6. Combine the butter, cinnamon powder, and baking powder in a mixing bowl.

7. Add the flour and thoroughly mix it up.

8. Combine the eggs and coffee in a mixing bowl.

9. Pour the yeast water into the mixing basin.

10. Stir in the remaining ingredients and combine well.

11. Transfer the batter to a baking dish.

12. Don't forget to grease the dish.

13. Place the dish in a big pan of water.

14. Check that the water level is lower than the dishes.

15. Bake the cake for 15 to 20 minutes.

Your dish is now ready to serve.

Recipe for Polish Blueberry Pierogi

Time to Prepare: 10 minutes

Time to cook: 40 minutes

2 servings

Ingredients:

1 cup blueberries

Yeast, for making dough

1 cup self-rising flour

1 teaspoon mixed spice

1 tablespoon milk

a teaspoon baking powder

There are two eggs.

a ½ cup of butter

1 cup brown sugar

Instructions:

1. Get a pan.

2. Pour in the butter.

3. Once it has melted, add the yeast and flour.

4. Combine the ingredients to make a dough.

5. Once the dough has formed, turn off the heat.

6. Pour the mixture into a mixing basin.

7. Combine the remaining ingredients in a mixing basin.

8. Combine all ingredients and shape the dough into the desired shapes.

9. Bake the mixture for 15 to 20 minutes.

10. Arrange the blueberries on top.

11. Your dish is now ready to serve.

Recipe for Polish Plum Cake

Time to Prepare: 50 minutes

Time to cook: 30 minutes

4 servings

Ingredients:

ten plums, fresh

1 tablespoon soy sauce, thin

1 tablespoon cinnamon powder

1 tablespoon white sugar

one spoonful of sweet vinegar

1 tablespoon brown powder

1 cup of milk

1 tablespoon vegetable oil

1 cup all-purpose flour

1/2 cup whole wheat flour

Season with salt to taste.

Kneed in water

1 teaspoon yeast

Instructions:

1. Get a bowl.

2. Stir in the flour.

3. Finally, add the yeast and sugar.

4. Pour in lukewarm water.

5. Set aside for 30 minutes.

6. Place the whole wheat flour in a separate basin.

7. Stir in the yeast dough.

Then, add the salt and some water.

9. Finally, combine the ingredients to make a soft dough.

Ten minutes of kneeling.

11. In the meantime, slice the plums.

12 Combine soy sauce, sweet vinegar, sugar, and salt.

13. Using the oil, shape the dough into round shapes.

14 Arrange the plum slices on top.

15 Bake the cake for 10 minutes.

Your dish is now ready to serve.

Recipe for Polish Rogaliki

Time to Prepare: 50 minutes

Time to cook: 30 minutes

4 servings

Ingredients:

2 cups almond flour

five tablespoons jam

1/2 teaspoon dried yeast

1 tablespoon white sugar

one spoonful of sweet vinegar

1 tablespoon brown powder

1 cup of milk

1 tablespoon vegetable oil

1 cup all-purpose flour

1/2 cup whole wheat flour

Season with salt to taste.

Kneed in water

5 tablespoons yogurt

Instructions:

1. Get a bowl.

2. Stir in the flour.

3. Finally, stir in the yeast and jam.

4. Pour in lukewarm water.

5. Set aside for 30 minutes.

6. Measure out the whole wheat flour.

7. Pour in some salt and water.

8. Combine the remaining ingredients to make a soft dough.

9. I kneeled for fifteen minutes.

10. Cut the pastries into the desired form.

11 Bake the pastries for 10 minutes at 350°F.

12. Your dish is now ready to serve.

Recipe for Polish Plum Dumplings

Time to Prepare: 40 minutes

Time to cook: 30 minutes

4 servings

Ingredients:

ten plums, fresh

1 tablespoon white sugar

one spoonful of sweet vinegar

1 tablespoon brown powder

1 cup of milk

a single egg

1 tablespoon vegetable oil

1 cup all-purpose flour

1/2 cup whole wheat flour

Season with salt to taste.

Kneed in water

1 teaspoon yeast

Instructions:

1. Get a bowl.

2. Pour the vegetable oil into the mixing bowl.

3. Stir in the white and brown sugars.

4. Gently mix it together to dissolve the sugar.

5. Pour in the all-purpose flour and milk.

6. Combine the yeast and salt in a mixing bowl.

7. The dough will be semi-soft.

8. Shape the dumplings from the mixture as desired.

9. Beat the eggs to make the egg mixture.

10. Dredge the dumplings in the egg mixture.

11 Cook the dumplings for 20 minutes.

12. Your dish is now ready to serve.

Recipe for Polish Apple Pie

Time to Prepare: 30 minutes

Time to cook: 50 minutes

4 servings

Ingredients:

Two apples

1 cup pie dough

a quarter cup wheat starch

2 tablespoons vegetable oil

2 cups brown sugar

1/2 teaspoon cinnamon powder

One-quarter cup whole milk

1/2 cup baking powder

Instructions:

1. Get a bowl.

2. Pour the vegetable oil into the mixing bowl.

3. Stir in the white and brown sugars.

4. Gently mix it and dissolve the sugar.

5. Pour the milk into the mixing bowl.

6. Gently fold in the apple slices.

7. Cut the pie dough into the appropriate shapes and bake the pies.

8. Fold the apple mixture into the pie crust.

9. Sprinkle with cinnamon.

Bake the pies for 50 minutes.

11. Your dish is now ready to serve.

Recipe for Polish Kolanchi Cookies

Time to Prepare: 10 minutes

Time to cook: 20 minutes

2 servings

Ingredients:

1 cup self-rising flour

1 tablespoon milk

a teaspoon baking powder

There are two eggs.

a ½ cup of butter

1 cup white sugar

1 tbsp cinnamon

1 teaspoon yeast

Instructions:

1. Place the butter in a medium mixing basin.

2. Stir in one cup of flour.

3. Pour warm milk into a separate basin.

4. Stir in the sugar and salt to the milk.

5. Combine the heated milk and flour mixture.

6. Combine the yeast, eggs, baking powder, and cinnamon.

7. For a few minutes, stir the mixture.

8. Shape the cookies any way you want.

Bake the cookies for 20 minutes.

10. Your dish is now ready to serve.

Recipe for Polish Babka Cake

Time to Prepare: 10 minutes

Time to cook: 40 minutes

2 servings

Ingredients:

1 cup powdered sugar

1 cup bittersweet chocolate

One cup of sugar

1 tsp vanilla extract

There are two eggs.

1 cup salted butter

1 cup walnut pieces

1 and ½ cups all-purpose flour

Instructions:

1. Get a bowl.

2. Place the salted butter in the mixing bowl.

3. Place the chocolate chunks in the bowl.

4. In a separate bowl, combine the sugar and eggs.

5. Combine the eggs and powdered sugar in a mixing bowl.

6. Pour the chocolate mixture into the chocolate bowl.

7. Stir in the vanilla essence and all-purpose flour.

8. Transfer the mixture to a baking dish.

9. Check that the dish is well-greased.

ten. Bake the cake for 25 minutes.

11. Serve the babka cake.

12 Cut them into desired shapes and sprinkle with powdered sugar on top.

13. Your meal is now ready to serve.

Recipe for Polish Glazed Pastry

Time to Prepare: 10 minutes

Time to cook: 15 minutes

2 servings

Ingredients:

2 cups almond flour

5 tablespoons jam

½ teaspoon dried yeast

1 tablespoon white sugar

one spoonful of sweet vinegar

1 tablespoon brown powder

1 cup of milk

1 tablespoon vegetable oil

1 cup all-purpose flour

½ cup whole wheat flour

Season with salt to taste.

Kneed in water

5 tablespoons yogurt

Instructions:

1. Place the almond flour in a mixing basin.

2. Stir in the yeast and jam.

3. Pour in lukewarm water.

4. Set aside for 30 minutes.

5. Place the whole wheat flour in a separate basin.

6. Stir in the yeast dough.

7. Pour in the salt and some water.

8. Finally, combine the ingredients to make a soft dough.

9. I kneeled for fifteen minutes.

10. Combine soy sauce, sweet vinegar, sugar, and salt.

11. Using the oil, shape the pastry into circular shapes.

12 Bake the pastries for 10 minutes.

13. Before baking, dip pastries in an egg mixture.

14. Your dish is now ready to serve.

Recipe for Polish Cream Pie Squares

Time to Prepare: 30 minutes

Time to cook: 10 minutes

4 servings

Ingredients:

two cups milk

two apple slices

1 tbsp cinnamon

½ cup heavy cream

½ cup white sugar

1 teaspoon salt

There are two eggs.

One teaspoon lemon essence

1 teaspoon almond extract

2 cups all-purpose flour

1 cup melted butter

Instructions:

1. Place the apples (sliced) in a medium bowl.

2. Stir in the heavy cream and cinnamon.

3. Stir in one cup of flour.

4. Place it in the refrigerator.

5. Place the butter in a large mixing bowl.

6. Stir in the sugar, salt, and milk.

7. Combine them thoroughly.

8. Combine the flour and the heated milk mixture.

9. Combine the eggs, lemon extract, and almond extract.

10. Continue to stir for a few minutes.

11 Cut the prepared material into square pies.

12. Bake the pies for 20 minutes or until they are slightly golden.

13. Your meal is now ready to serve.

Recipe for Sernik (Polish Cheesecake).

Time to Prepare: 10 minutes

Time to cook: 10 minutes

4 servings

Ingredients:

two cups milk

1 cup shredded cheese

1 tablespoon baking powder

Yeast, 1 cup

1/2 cup white sugar

1 teaspoon salt

There are two eggs.

One teaspoon lemon essence

1 teaspoon almond extract

2 cups all-purpose flour

1 cup melted butter

Instructions:

1. Place the cheese in a medium mixing basin.

2. Stir in one cup of flour.

3. Pour milk into a large mixing bowl.

4. Add the sugar and salt to taste.

5. Combine them thoroughly.

6. Combine the heated milk mixture, flour, and yeast.

7. Combine the eggs, lemon extract, and almond extract.

8. Continue to stir for a few minutes.

9. Bake the cake for 15 to 20 minutes.

10. Your dish is now ready to serve.

Recipe for Piernik (Polish Gingerbread)

Time to Prepare: 30 minutes

Time to cook: 10 minutes

2 servings

Ingredients:

1 cup almond flour

2 teaspoons ginger powder

½ cup brown sugar

½ cup baking powder

a half cup of milk

a pinch salt

1 tbsp. almond extract

Instructions:

1. In a mixing dish, combine one cup of flour and ginger powder.

2. Combine them thoroughly.

3. Pour the heavy cream into a separate large mixing bowl.

4. Stir in the sugar, salt, and milk.

5. Combine them thoroughly.

6. In the bowl of milk, combine the eggs and almond essence.

7. Transfer the ginger powder mixture to the second mixing bowl.

8. Combine all of the ingredients thoroughly.

9. Combine all of the ingredients in a baking dish.

10. Bake for ten minutes with the ingredients.

11. Your dish is now ready to serve.

Recipe for Polish Plesniak Cake

Time to Prepare: 15 minutes

Time to cook: 25 minutes

3 servings

Ingredients:

two cups milk

1 tablespoon cocoa powder

1/2 cup white sugar

1 teaspoon salt

There are two eggs.

One teaspoon lemon essence

1 teaspoon almond extract

2 cups all-purpose flour

1 cup melted butter

1 teaspoon dry yeast

Instructions:

1. Place the butter in a medium mixing basin.

2. Stir in 1 cup of flour.

3. Place the mixture in the refrigerator.

4. Pour yeast into a separate big mixing dish.

5. Stir in the sugar, salt, and milk.

6. Combine them thoroughly.

7. Combine the heated milk and flour mixture.

8. Combine the eggs, lemon extract, and almond extract.

9. Continue to stir for a few minutes.

10. Stir in the cocoa powder to the mixture.

11. Bake the cake for 25 minutes or until it turns a light brown hue.

12. Your dish is now ready to serve.

Recipe for Polish Walnut Kiflies

Time to Prepare: 30 minutes

Time to cook: 10 minutes

4 servings

Ingredients:

1 cup all-purpose flour

1 cup cream cheese

a ½ cup of butter

a half cup of sugar

1 cup baking powder

1 teaspoon rum extract

1 cup of milk

One tablespoon of vanilla extract

1 cup heavy cream

½ cup walnuts

Instructions:

1. Place the butter and cream cheese in a medium mixing bowl.

2. Stir in the yeast and one cup of flour.

3. Combine them thoroughly.

4. Once the dough has been prepared, cut out the kiflles of your choice.

5. Pour the heavy cream into a large mixing basin.

6. Stir in the sugar, salt, and milk.

7. Combine them thoroughly.

8. Incorporate the baking powder into the mixture.

9. Combine the eggs and vanilla essence.

10. Continue to stir for a few minutes.

11. Apply the prepared mixture to the kiflles.

12. Sprinkle the chopped walnuts over the kifles.

13 Bake for 10 minutes.

14. Your dish is now ready to serve.

Recipe for Polish Easter Babka

Time to Prepare: 50 minutes

Time to cook: 10 minutes

4 servings

Ingredients:

1 cup chocolate syrup

1 tablespoon cocoa powder

2 cups melted butter

½ cup warm water

1 cup caster sugar

There are two eggs.

½ cup rice flour

1 tablespoon oil

Season with salt to taste.

Coffee pins, as needed

Instructions:

1. Fill a dish with four cups of water.

2. Bring the water to a boil.

3. Combine the cocoa powder, chocolate syrup, and sugar in a mixing bowl.

4. Bring the water to a boil until all ingredients are dissolved.

5. Combine the sugar and oil in a mixing bowl.

6. Turn off the heat once a consistent mixture has been generated.

7. Sift flour into a large mixing bowl.

8. Stir in the eggs.

9. Combine the eggs and flour.

10. Combine the chocolate syrup mixture and the remaining ingredients in a mixing dish.

11. Gently fold the mixture to produce a dough structure.

12 Form the mixture into small round balls and lay them on a baking sheet.

13. Bake for ten minutes.

14. Your dish is now ready to serve.

Recipe for Polish Lemon Babka

Time to Prepare: 50 minutes

Time to cook: 10 minutes

4 servings

Ingredients:

1 cup lemon syrup

2 cups lemon curd

2 cups melted butter

½ cup warm water

1 cup caster sugar

½ cup rice flour

1 tablespoon oil

Season with salt to taste.

Half cup oats

1 tablespoon lemon zest

½ cup lemon juice

Instructions:

1. Fill a dish with four cups of water.

2. Bring the water to a boil.

3. Combine the lemon zest, syrup, and sugar in a mixing bowl.

4. Bring the water to a boil until all ingredients are dissolved.

5. Combine the sugar and oil in a mixing bowl.

6. Turn off the heat when the mixture is homogeneous.

7. Sift flour into a large mixing bowl.

8. Stir in the eggs.

9. Combine the eggs and flour.

10. Combine the remaining ingredients in a mixing basin.

11. Pour the lemon syrup mixture into the mixing bowl.

12. Gently fold the mixture to produce a dough structure.

13. Shape the mixture into small round balls and lay them on a baking sheet.

14 Bake for 10 minutes at 350°F.

15. Your dish is now ready to serve.

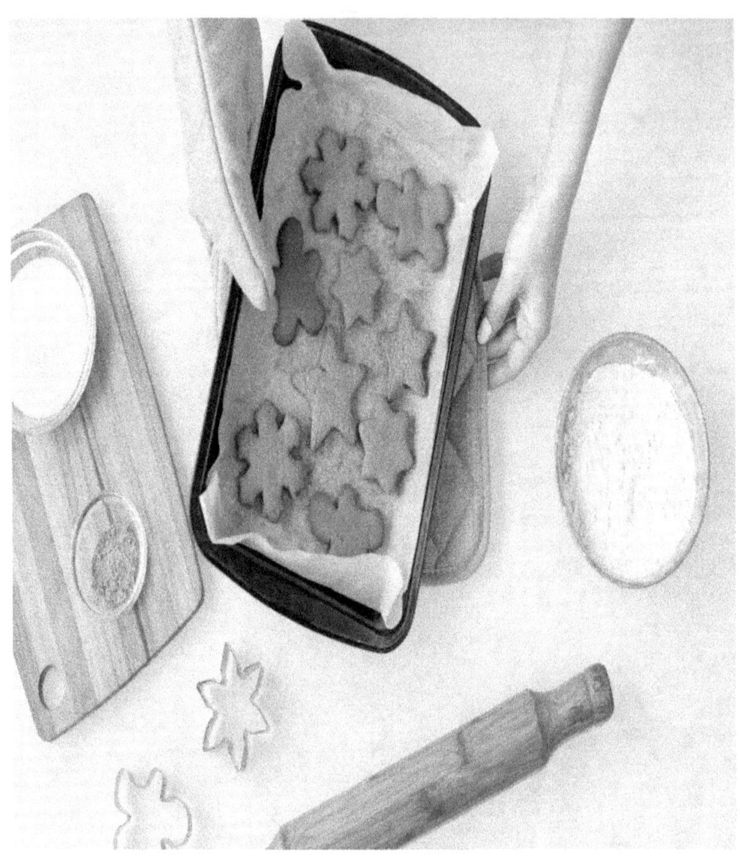

The World of Polish Snack Recipes, Chapter 6

The following are some traditional Polish snack foods that are high in nutritious elements and are simple to prepare thanks to the full directions provided in each recipe:

Recipe for Polish Spiced Honey Bread

Time to Prepare: 15 minutes

Time to cook: 30 minutes

3 servings

Ingredients:

2 tablespoons of caster sugar

½ cup of honey

½ spoonful of ground cloves

1 tbsp cinnamon

1 tablespoon nutmeg

½ cup unsalted butter

There are two eggs.

½ cup cream of tartar

2 cups all-purpose flour

Icing sugar, for dusting

Instructions:

1. Fill a big pan halfway with water.

2. Warm it up over medium-high heat.

3. Stir in the sugar.

4. Cook till golden caramel.

5. Combine the honey, cinnamon, cloves, and nutmeg in a mixing bowl.

6. Increase the heat to high and cook for 5 minutes.

7. Remove from the fire and set aside to cool.

Take a big mixing bowl.

9. Stir in the cream of tartar and flour.

10. Stir in the butter, eggs, and seasoned sugar.

11 Stir it until a dough forms.

12. Once the dough has been prepared, shape the bread into the desired shape.

13 Bake the dough for 15 minutes.

14. Your dish is now ready to serve.

Recipe for Polish Sweet Cheese Buns

Time to Prepare: 30 minutes
Time to cook: 35 minutes

5 servings

Ingredients:

2 cups ricotta cheese

½ cup golden raisins

1 box of yeast

There are 2 eggs.

Milk,

2 cups all-purpose flour

Water, as needed

1 tablespoon lime zest

1 cup vegetable oil

1 cup bottled water

Instructions:

1. Place the flour in a large mixing bowl.

2. Pour in the supplied yeast.

3. Pour the yeast into the water.

4. Stir in the sugar.

5. Stir in the eggs, lemon zest, and milk.

6. Mix the dough for another ten minutes.

7. Place the dough in an oiled mixing bowl.

8. Roll out the dough and cut it into squares.

9. Fill each square with cheese and fold the dough.

10. Arrange the squares on a prepared baking sheet.

11. Spoon the remaining egg mixture and lime zest over the buns.

12 Cook the buns for 30 minutes.

13. Remove the buns when they have turned golden brown.

14. Your dish is now ready to serve.

Recipe for Kielbasal (Polish Hush Puppies).

Time to prepare: 20 minutes

Time to cook: 20 minutes

2 servings

Ingredients:

1 cup cornmeal

2 cups all-purpose flour

1 tablespoon sugar

1 tablespoon salt

Cooking oil, as needed

½ teaspoon baking soda

1 tablespoon ground black pepper

2 tablespoons butter

1 cup plain yogurt

1 cup sauerkraut

1 cup Cheddar cheese

1 onion, chopped

Instructions:

1. Take a large mixing dish.

2. Stir in the sauerkraut and onions.

3. Stir in the cheddar cheese.

4. Combine everything thoroughly.

5. Get a new bowl.

6. Combine the cornmeal, flour, salt, sugar, baking soda, and black pepper in a mixing bowl.

7. Thoroughly combine them.

8. Stir in the butter, yogurt, and egg.

9. To the second bowl, add the sauerkraut mixture.

10. Form round balls and deep-fried them in hot oil till golden brown.

11. Your dish is now ready to serve.

Grzanki Polish Recipe

Time to Prepare: 5 minutes

Time to cook: 10 minutes

3 servings

Ingredients:

4 bread pieces

4 tablespoons tomato sauce

½ cup cooked mushrooms

½ cup shredded mozzarella

Instructions:

1. Cut the bread into the desired size slices.

2. Drizzle with tomato sauce.

3. Add the mushrooms on top.

4. Evenly distribute the mozzarella cheese across the bread slices.

5. Bake the bread pieces for 5–10 minutes.

6. Remove the bread slices when they have turned golden brown.

7. Your dish is now ready to serve.

Recipe for Polish Nachos

Time to Prepare: 15 minutes

Time to cook: 10 minutes

4 servings

Ingredients:

2 tablespoons kielbasa sausage

1 onion

Sauerkraut, anyone?

½ cup of beer

½ cup Cheddar cheese

½ cup tortilla chips

1 pinch black pepper, ground

1 cup olive oil

a pinch salt

Instructions:

1. Bring the water to a boil in a saucepan.

2. Cook the kielbasa in a pan for 30 minutes.

3. Remove the kielbasa from the pan.

4. Allow to cool before slicing the kielbasa.

5. Preheat a second pan.

6. Pour the oil into the pan.

7. Add the onion and cook until softened.

8. Stir in the sauerkraut.

9. Stir in the beer and black pepper.

10. Stir in the kielbasa slices.

11. Allow the mixture to simmer for 10 minutes.

12. Stir in the cheddar cheese.

13. Arrange the tortilla chips on a plate.

14 Arrange the tortilla chips on top of the kielbasa mixture.

15. Your dish is now ready to serve.

Recipe for Polish Prunes Wrapped in Bacon

Time to prepare: 20 minutes

Time to cook: 15 minutes

4 servings

Ingredients:

5 slices of bacon

10 prunes

For greasing, use butter.

Season with salt to taste.

Black pepper, as desired

As needed, chopped cilantro

Instructions:

1. Place the Prunes in a mixing dish.

2. Pour in the boiling water.

3. After ten minutes, drain the prunes.

4. Roll the prunes in bacon slices.

5. Spread butter on the prunes.

6. Sprinkle with salt and pepper.

7. Bake for 5 minutes with the prunes.

8. Bake the prunes until the bacon is crisp.

9. Garnish with chopped cilantro.

10. Your dish is now ready to serve.

Recipe for Polish Potato and Cheese Pierogi

Time to Prepare: 30 minutes

Time to cook: 30 minutes

4 servings

Ingredients:

Season with salt to taste.

Black pepper, as desired

1 bag of dumpling dough

1 cup sour cream

1 cup chopped chives

1 cup chopped potatoes

½ cup mozzarella cheese

2 tbsp garlic mince

Horseradish, 2 tbsp

½ cup chopped parsley

2 tbsp olive oil

Instructions:

1. Take a large mixing dish.

2. Stir in the sour cream.

3. Beat the ingredients together until frothy.

4. Stir in the potatoes, mozzarella cheese, minced garlic, and horseradish.

5. Combine all of the ingredients thoroughly.

6. Season with salt and pepper to taste.

7. Make the dumpling dough.

8. Cut circles out of the dough and fill them with the mixture.

9. Roll up the dumplings.

10. Place the dumplings in a big saucepan with boiling water.

11. Cook the pierogi for 5 minutes before draining.

12. Cook the dumplings in olive oil until golden brown on both sides.

13. Plate the pierogi and top with chopped parsley leaves.

14. Your dish is now ready to serve.

Recipe for Polish Zapiekanka (Pizza).

Time to Prepare: 5 minutes

Time to cook: 30 minutes

3 servings

Ingredients:

2 tbsp caraway seeds

1 tablespoon olive oil

Two sweet onions

1 cup shredded cheese

1 cup sauerkraut

Kielbasa in a single packet

1 teaspoon red chili pepper

1 pack pizza crust

Black pepper, as desired

Instructions:

1. Preheat the oven to 350°F.

2. Place the pizza crust on a baking sheet.

3. Sprinkle the caraway seeds on top of the dough.

4. In a separate pan, add the onions.

5. Cook for 10 minutes or until the onions begin to caramelize.

6. Cook for another 10 minutes after adding the kielbasa.

7. Spread the kielbasa mixture on top of the pizza crust.

8. Sprinkle the cheese over the kielbasa mixture.

9. Sprinkle the red chili pepper on top of the cheese.

10. Bake the pizza for the remaining ten minutes.

11. Your dish is now ready to serve.

Recipe for Polish Apple Fritters

Time to Prepare: 30 minutes

Time to cook: 10 minutes

4 servings

Ingredients:

1 cup of milk

There are two eggs.

1 teaspoon salt

1 cup all-purpose flour

1 tablespoon baking powder

two apples, chopped

1 cup vegetable oil

Add sugar to taste.

Instructions:

1. In a blender, combine the milk, eggs, and flour.

2. Stir in the salt and baking powder.

3. Combine all of the ingredients.

4. Finally, stir in the diced apples.

5. Combine everything thoroughly.

6. In a skillet, heat the oil.

7. Fry the prepared ingredients in tiny fritters.

8. Cook until the fritters are golden brown.

9. Your dish is now ready to serve.

Recipe for Polish Lard Spread

Time to prepare: 20 minutes

Time to cook: 30 minutes

2 servings

Ingredients:

Leaf fat, as needed

2 onions

2 cloves garlic

2 apples, chopped

½ cup chopped bacon

2 tablespoons pepper

1 tablespoon salt

1 teaspoon marjoram

Instructions:

1. Grind the leaves card and place it in a big skillet.

2. Thoroughly cook the lard mixture.

3. To the skillet, add the onion, garlic, and diced bacon.

4. Stir in the chopped apples, salt, and pepper.

5. Incorporate the marjoram into the mixture.

6. Turn off the heat when the mixture thickens.

7. Spread the spread on rye bread and serve.

Recipe for Polish Cheese Spread with Radish

Time to Prepare: 15 minutes

Time to cook: 5 minutes

2 servings

Ingredients:

1 cup cottage cheese

1 radish

Season with salt to taste.

1 tablespoon garlic powder

to taste, black pepper

1 onion

As needed, bread slices

Instructions:

1. Melt the cheese in a big skillet.

2. Once the cheese has melted, add the onion, garlic, and radish slices.

3. Season with salt and pepper.

4. After a few seconds, turn off the stove.

5. Place the bread slices on top of the mixture.

6. Your dish is now ready to serve.

Conclusion

Polish cuisine is well-known for its variety of tasty, spicy, and filling meals prepared locally and in neighboring countries. Poland provides a taste of Europe's distinctive cuisine, from delectable doughnuts to filling dumplings and succulent pork. We examined the recipes and several aspects of Polish cookery in this book. We went over the history and origins of Polish foods in great depth. The numerous substances used in Polish cookery provide a plethora of excellent health benefits. This cookbook has 77 breakfast, lunch, supper, dessert, and snack dishes. You can create these dishes at home without any supervision. So start cooking today and have fun making Polish food at home.